A PERSONAL PRAYER BOOK

PERSONAL PRAYERS FOR GROWING CHRISTIANS

> A Gift From Colonial Park Church
> 430 Colonial Road
> Harrisburg, PA 17109
> 717-545-1911

ALLAN W. SCHREIBER

DIMENSIONS
FOR LIVING
NASHVILLE

Morning   Day 1

Good morning, Lord! I thank you that I belong to you and that I am making my journey through life in your company and with many fellow saints as my brothers and sisters.

What a privilege it is for me to be called one of your saints, even though I have done nothing to deserve such an honored title. I know this is my privilege because Jesus lived a perfect life for me, and because all my sin is washed away by his precious blood. By faith in Jesus I am a forgiven sinner, and that's why I am a saint of God.

Lord, Help me live today in the knowledge that Jesus is really living in me, so that—
   my reaction to what others do to me will reflect Christ's love and forgiveness;
   I will be more kind and gracious to others;
   I will control my feelings and recall who I am before I do anything hasty;
   I may live through this day doing my best in all things.

May this day be a good day for me and for all God's people. I ask this in Jesus' name. Amen.

Evening   Day 1

Dear Lord in heaven, it is so good to think of you before I sleep. When I was a young child, it seemed much easier to remember to say my prayers before I went to sleep; I would say: "Now I lay me down to sleep" or some other prayers quite regularly. But now I am ashamed to say that quite often I simply fall asleep before I talk to you. Forgive me when I forget, and help me always to remember to talk with you before I "lay me down to sleep."

I want to say thank you, Lord, for all the good things that happened today.
(Pause here and list those good things.)

Thank you, too, for the things that did not go so well, for which I know I was at least partly to blame. Please forgive me now, and wash away all my sins with the precious blood of Jesus, which was poured out for us all on Calvary's cross. It is so wonderful to know that Jesus has made me right with God. Now I am clean. The past is wiped away. Tomorrow is a new day, a new beginning. Let me sleep in peace, for Jesus' sake. Amen.

Morning   Day 2

My dear Lord, as I begin a new day in my life, I want to thank you for your protection during the night. It is so comforting to realize that your angels were watching over me during the night, and I could sleep in safety and peace.

Help me to realize that today is your wonderful gift to me, another day to be used in giving glory to you and in helping others who look to me for love and kindness.

Help me to appreciate all that you give me each day, things that I often take for granted, such as the good food, strength, and health I enjoy; the clothes I wear; the good times I have with my family and friends, especially those in my church family.

Lord, I know there are many other people in the world who don't have half as much as you have given me. That thought this morning makes me truly thankful for all your gifts to me.

Give me the energy and enthusiasm to do my work well this day. I ask this in Jesus' name. Amen.

Evening   Day 2

Heavenly Lord, thank you for bringing me to the end of this day. Sometimes, at the end of a day, I feel rather weary and tired after I've worked hard. Please forgive me for the times I've forgotten to thank you for helping me cope with the ups and downs of life.

Lord, there are times when I get rather frustrated with my work and my life in general. I wonder whether I'm on the right road for my future, and whether it will turn out all right in the end.

Help me to talk to you as the most understanding One of all, a friend who I know is always more ready to listen than I am to speak or ask. And help me to listen when you speak in your Word to guide and direct me for what lies ahead.

Give me all I need to cope with the challenges of growing to be what you want me to be. I know you want me to be more like Jesus, and that is what I want to be, too.

Let me rest in peace as I sleep tonight. Amen.

Morning   Day 3

Dear Lord, last night came and went so quickly, and here I am starting a new day. Help me remember during this day that you are with me all the time. Prompt me to do the good things you've prepared for me to do and to avoid the wrong things that might tempt me today.

Lord, I want to grow as one of your special people,
> so I need your help—
> > to grow in faith, love, and trust;
> > to handle relationships with the members of my family and with other people at school or at work;
> > to realize that other people in our church family are also your dear saints, whom you want me to love as brothers and sisters;
> > to confess to my friends in the world that I am a Christian;
> > to be available to those who are looking for my friendship.

My Lord, you know me, and I know you can help me with your guidance and power. Help me to accept your help so that I may become the kind of person you want me to be.

Be with me now during this day so that no harm comes to me. I ask this in Jesus' name. Amen.

Evening　　　　　　　　　　　　Day 3

It is good to come to the end of another day of my life and quietly talk to you, my Lord and God.

During the day I don't always realize you are with me and in me, but deep down I know you are there. You have promised that you will never leave your loved ones, and I really appreciate that promise.

Help me to keep growing in the faith that always trusts you—even when things aren't going as well as I would like.

Give me—
   peace, as I go to rest, remembering that Jesus forgives my sins as I confess them to him;
   joy in knowing that I am already a member of God's heavenly kingdom, not because I have done so well, but because Jesus has given this to me as a gift;
   patience, as I wait for my own future to develop in this life and as I wait for the final coming of Jesus to give me his eternal glory.

I now go to sleep, relaxed in my body, mind, and spirit, in the name of the Father and of the Son and of the Holy Spirit. Amen.

Morning   Day 4

Lord, I've just begun a new day, your gift to me. Thank you for the sleep I enjoyed last night.

Help me be aware of your presence all through this day.

Help me—
- to live this day with complete confidence that through your gift of baptism I am your child;
- to keep growing in the gifts of the Holy Spirit, which you have poured out upon me;
- to realize that, even when I think I don't have many gifts, you will help me discover what gifts I have as I mature and grow in the fullness of Jesus;
- to cope with my weaknesses and frustrations, especially when I seem to keep falling into the same troubles again and again;
- to come back to you for your forgiveness as soon as I realize I've gone wrong;
- to live with real joy in knowing that your forgiveness releases me to develop my life as you have planned for me.

Lord, I trust in you to make this a good day for me. And I know you will give me all these things that I ask, for Jesus' sake. Amen.

Evening   Day 4

Dear Lord, another day is over, and I want to pause to talk with you for a little while before I go to sleep.

As I reflect upon this day, I realize—
> that much of the day went by so quickly that I wasn't aware of your presence—yet, Lord I know you were there;
> that not everything worked out as well as I had hoped;
> that I could have done some things better than I did;
> that I probably hurt someone's feelings without even realizing what I had done;
> that I've broken your laws and deserve your punishment;
> that you want me to face you as I really am, not just as I want others to see me.

But, Lord, I'm sorry that I've done things wrong or have forgotten to do some good things that I should have done. I call on Jesus to cover me with his perfection, for he has made all things right with God for me; and I ask for his forgiveness, provided for me by his death on the cross. Thank you, Lord, for Jesus. I will never cease to praise you for all you've done for me. In Jesus' precious name. Amen.

Morning   Day 5

O Lord, as I begin to talk with you this morning, I must first tell you how much I appreciate the refreshment of last night's sleep.

One day, I know, I shall come to my final rest on this earth; and, thanks to Jesus, I am ready. But, until that time comes, I want to face each new day eagerly. So I seek your blessing today as I go out to my work.

As I receive your blessing, I want you to bless others who also need your help, especially those—
who have no work and really feel rather useless;
who do have work but are not doing the work they really want to do;
who are struggling with problems that seem to have no solution;
who are not aware of the real meaning of life, and feel frustrated and depressed;
who are facing the end of life with no one to support them.

Lord, help these people through one of your saints, giving them your loving help;
and, if I am the one you are calling to give this help, let me hear and obey your call.

Watch over me now as I go my way. At the end of the day, may I feel that this day has been well spent. I ask this for Jesus' sake. Amen.

Evening   Day 5

My God, tonight I want to tell you just how easily I seem to get sidetracked and even hopelessly lost at times.

Sometimes I think I've got myself and my life sorted out, and then things go wrong again. As I look at my life, I'm ashamed of how often I go wrong in the same places over and over again. I often wonder if I'll ever get it right. Please forgive my failures as I now confess them to you.

I thank you, Lord, that Jesus didn't get lost as he went through his life on earth for us; otherwise, we would be lost forever. He must have felt terrible when faced with all our sin and with the pain and punishment we caused. It must have been hard for him to go straight on down the road to the cross. But he did go all the way for us. Then, even beyond the wildest hopes of all his disciples, he rose from the dead and showed us what victory he has won for us.

O God, fill me with glory, praise, love, and thankfulness for all that Jesus did for me.

With his spirit now resting on me, I go to rest in peace. In the blessed name of Jesus. Amen.

Morning   Day 6

Lord, some people find it easy to get going first thing in the morning, and others of us find it rather difficult. As this new day gets under way, give us all your power-boost for a good start.

Please help me during this day—
- to do my best in all my work;
- to be warm and pleasant as I mix with other people;
- to be thoughtful and helpful when I see others in need;
- to be more like the person you want me to be;
- to show proper respect to those whom I ought to respect, even when I find it difficult;
- to face cheerfully the rough patches this day may bring.

Direct my life so that at the end of this day I'll be able to look back with real pleasure and be able to say: "Thanks, loving God, for a really good day." Amen.

Evening   Day 6

It is good to go to bed at night knowing that all is right.

If there is anything on my conscience that has harmed my relationship with you and other people, dear God, please forgive me and remove all that is wrong.

As I go to rest, assure me again that all is right with you. If I had to depend on my own goodness and efforts to be made right with you, I know I would never be right. I am so thankful to you, my God, that you gave Jesus to be perfect on our behalf and to undergo all the pain, suffering, and death that should have been our punishment. When Jesus covers me with his life, death, and resurrection, I am sure that I am right with you, dear God—and that is the most important thing in my life.

As I fall asleep, let me feel your arms surrounding me, so that I can rest in real peace. I join with St. Paul who expressed his great faith in the words: "Whether we live or die, we belong to the Lord" (Rom. 14:8).

This I pray in Jesus' name. Amen.

Morning   Day 7

This morning, heavenly Lord, I want you to give me a right attitude and spirit so I can do things well today. Help me look forward cheerfully to what I must do today so that I complete my work faithfully.

Help me speak to people kindly so that they may enjoy my company. Help me deal with frustrations, disappointments, and opposition with the peace and calmness that comes from you, so that I will not become irritated at myself or other people. Help me reflect the great love of Jesus in helping others whenever I sense that they are hurting and are in need.

When people pay me compliments, help me to be humble, remembering that all the praise and glory belong to you, O God.

Give me and all people your blessing as we go out to meet this new day. I pray this with real confidence in your unchanging love. Amen.

Evening   Day 7

As I come to the end of another day, it is time to take off my clothes, get ready for bed, and go to sleep. That reminds me how I need to take off the old sinful human nature, and to put on the new nature, which has been mine ever since my baptism.

Lord, my old nature gives me a lot of trouble at times—
> Words come out of my mouth that I should never say;
> anger grows in my heart that should not be there;
> feelings of rebellion and disobedience make me difficult to live with;
> forbidden pleasures seem so attractive and exciting.

Help me now to confess my faults; please forgive my failures, and make me clean with the blood of my Savior Jesus. Let his good qualities take control of my life, so that my life is pleasing to you, and I become the kind of person who is easy to live with.

I ask these things before I go to rest tonight, knowing that in Jesus my prayer is heard and answered. Amen.

Morning　　　　　　　　　　　Day 8

Dear God, this is the day you have made for us to enjoy. Some days seem to fly, while others just drag on. I pray that this day will not be boring, but will be filled with activities and experiences that are interesting.

Help me—
- to have a positive attitude to the things that will happen during this day;
- to have a pleasant smile for those with whom I work or study—even if I find it hard to be friendly toward them;
- to do my best so that you will be pleased with my work, and others as well;
- to see the needs of those around me and to meet those needs without being asked.

Dear God, you have a plan for me and my life, but at times I wonder if I'm on the right track. Give me the confidence that through all my varied experiences you are guiding me to discover and do you will for my life.

Help me realize that every moment of this day is also part of your plan for me. Then I will be able to accept and enjoy what comes my way.

This I ask for Jesus' sake. Amen.

Evening   Day 8

The days simply fly by, and so many things happen in one day. To me it seems that most people are just rushing about filling up the days of their lives with trivial things and without even thinking about you, God.

Yet I sometimes wonder if our lives do depend on what we plan and do. Maybe you don't exist at all. Maybe you don't have any control over us. Maybe the Bible is not really your Word to us.

O God, when I have such doubts, my first thought is the fear that you might strike me off your list for having such doubts. But then I remember that many great saints in your kingdom have also had doubts. How comforting to know that, when Thomas could not believe that Jesus had risen from the dead, our Savior did not reject him, but led him to renewed faith and certainty.

As I go to sleep tonight, give me the certainty that overcomes all doubts. Strengthen my faith, and give me the comforting assurance of your presence, so that I, like Thomas, can fall down before my Savior and say: "My Lord and my God!" Then I will sleep in peace and rise renewed for the challenges of another day. Amen.

Morning   Day 9

Dear Lord, sometimes I ask myself why I take the trouble to speak to you. But then I know it is because your Holy Spirit has entered my life and has lived in me ever since my baptism. Through water and the Word, he gave me my new birth, so that I am your born-again child. I can now call you "Dear Father," and that is why I want to talk to you day by day.

Forgive me for those times when I forget to keep in touch with you—
> by not reading and meditating on your Word at home,
> by not hearing your Word in church,
> and by not availing myself of Holy Communion.

Help me to remember that only those led by the Spirit of God are true children of God. Give me even more power from your Holy Spirit, so that I daily live in both the comfort and the challenge of my baptism.

Give your special blessing to your people everywhere, especially to those whom I love, my friends, my family, and the people beside whom I work.

We are your children in Jesus. Give your blessing to us as we begin this new day in your name. Amen.

Evening   Day 9

This morning in my prayers, my God, I thought about my baptism, and how you accepted me into your kingdom by the power of your Spirit. Since that time, thanks to parents, godparents, pastors, Sunday school teachers, and other Christians, my faith in Jesus as my Savior and the Lord of my life has grown. And I pray that it will remain strong, and grow even stronger, until the end of my life.

Lord, you are the potter, and I am the clay in your wise and loving hands. Continue to mold me according to your will. Make me clean in Jesus, and help me grow to be more like him. Fill me with the Spirit's gifts that will help me to become what I already am in Jesus. Help me to become more aware of how you are doing this in my life day by day.

Before I go to rest, I ask for your special blessing on all who are thinking of me and praying for me tonight, especially my own family, friends, and loved ones.

Bless those who have no one to remember them, and no one to pray for them, and for whom tonight will be terribly lonely. I pray this as your child in Jesus Christ. Amen.

Morning   Day 10

When we are young, Lord, it is easy to imagine that life just goes on day after day forever.

It's hard to believe that one day we'll be old—and even harder to think that this life will come to an end. When we hear about the death of someone who was still very young, remind us that death comes to all of us as you know best, to some when they are quite young and to others when they are very old.

As I think about the end of life, help me realize the importance of being right with you. Thank you so much for Jesus who has given me the guarantee that I am one of your saints, living with God now, and ready to live in glory forever.

As one of your saints, today I want—
- to be humble so that others will find me easy to live with;
- to be in control of my feelings and my words so that I won't offend anyone or say things that are unkind;
- to be patient at all times so that I don't irritate others;
- to be faithful so that I don't let others down.

These are the spiritual gifts I would like to have today. For Jesus' sake. Amen.

Evening   Day 10

Now the day is over, night is drawing near.
    Sometime I find the darkness is still a bit scary.

Dear God, you've told us in your Word that to live
    without you is like living in complete darkness.
    And so it is very true that to live in darkness
    without you is very frightening.

How thankful I am that I am not living in that darkness,
    so that there is never any need for me really to
      feel scared.
    Jesus said: "I am the light of the world";
    and since I am living in Jesus, I am living in
      the light.

Tonight I want to thank you, God, for all the help
    you've given me during today.

Thank you for—
    keeping me safe from all danger;
    helping me carry out today's tasks;
    keeping me safe with Jesus, preventing me from
      being led astray;
    giving me many wonderful friends and caring
      fellow Christians.

Help me lie down with a happy and peaceful heart. I
    ask this through Jesus Christ my Lord. Amen.

Morning   Day 11

Lord, another day has dawned. Like so many days before this, I guess there will be situations when things will go well and times when there will be trouble. When troubles come my way, please give me lots of patience and self-control so that I don't become too upset or raise my voice in anger and hurt others.

When the course of the day runs smoothly, help me to be thankful and realize that it is because your hand is guiding me that life goes well.

Help me during today to do your will by—
 giving comfort to those who are hurting;
 offering a smile to those who are sad;
 being a friend to the lonely;
 giving encouragement to the downhearted;
 sharing the good news of Jesus whenever I have the chance.

Make this day a good day for me and all people. For Jesus' sake. Amen.

Evening

Day 11

This day is drawing to a close; it will never return.
>   Lord, as I look back over today, I want to ask your forgiveness for—
>   not using all its hours as wisely as possible;
>   not working as hard as I could have;
>   not listening to the calls for help around me;
>   not sharing my time with friends and loved ones;
>   being too busy to remember the claims of my home, my church family, and my community;
>   being too absorbed in myself that I forget to look up and see your beauty in this world.

Lord, I thank you that when you forgive me, you wipe my sins from your memory. Watch over this world as we go to sleep. Bless your loved ones and refresh your weary ones as we sleep in peace. In Jesus' name I pray. Amen.

Morning　　　　　　　　　　　Day 12

Good morning, dear Lord in heaven! One of the psalmists wrote: "As the deer pants for streams of water, so my soul pants for you, O God. My soul thirsts for God, for the living God" (Ps. 42:1-2).

There are times when I say those words with real feeling and meaning. But would you understand if I confess that there are many times in my life when I'm not so aware of any real thirst for you? I know the reason for failing to long for you: My old human nature is still alive in me and tries to get me to forget you entirely.

But how thankful I am, dear God, that today, as I face a new day, I also know that you have graciously made me a new creation in Christ, blessed with a new nature, through your Holy Spirit.

Let that new life control all I think, say, or do today, so that I seek to please you in everything;
I do my work as well as I can;
I overcome temptation in the power of Christ my Lord;
I take my responsibilities seriously;
I share my love with my friends and with those who miss out on so much in life.

I ask this for your love's sake. Amen.

Evening   Day 12

O Lord, what do I want to say to you at the end of another day?

First of all, I want to say thank you for all the good things that happened today—
> for every opportunity to do the things that please you;
> for the acts of kindness and love that made me happy:
>> those that others did for me,
>> and those that I was able to do for them;
>
> for the fun and pleasure that I enjoyed with other people, especially in my own home.

Next, I want to say I'm sorry—
> for all the mistakes and failures of today;
> for failing to say thank you to those who did so much for me;
> for anything I said or did that hurt anyone's feelings;
>
> for behaving as if I am the most unfairly treated, misunderstood person in this world.

Finally, give me your forgiveness before I go to sleep. Because of Jesus, I know the past can be left behind; I can sleep in peace and can look forward to a new day with you tomorrow.

I pray all this confidently in Jesus' name. Amen.

Morning　　　　　　　　　　Day 13

In the morning when I am physically and spiritually still drowsy, Holy Spirit, I ask you to wake me and to refresh me with your gifts in my body, mind, and spirit.

I know that you are living and working in me, making me new each day, reminding me that I am God's very own person, giving me power to keep growing like Jesus, helping me see God's will during each day that I live, and strengthening me to do it obediently.

Today especially, Holy Spirit, continue to help me and all Christians keep growing in faith and Christlike living.

Spirit of God, give me wisdom—
- to be alert to any dangers that could hurt me, and to avoid them;
- to know when I should speak and when I should be silent;
- to see the needs of people around me, and to meet those needs as best I can;
- to grasp opportunities for sharing the joy of knowing Jesus, and to do so humbly.

This is my prayer this morning, in Jesus' name. Amen.

Evening   Day 13

As I review my past day, I recall such a variety of happenings: some good, some not so good—and some things I'd rather not talk about.

Even though I sometimes have doubts, I know, dear God, that your Word says that all things work for good for those who love you. So I know that all that happened today was really for my good—even those things that now make me feel rather ashamed.

So that today's faults and failures may be for my good, remind me again—
- that I dare not stand before you in pride, with any spiritual goodness of my own;
- that free forgiveness is available through the cross of Jesus to wipe away all my sin;
- that the Holy Spirit is at my side to help me fight the good fight of faith and make fewer mistakes next time.

Let your holy angels watch over me and all my loved ones as we go to sleep. Sure of your love and care because we are your children through Jesus, we can truly sleep in peace. Amen.

Morning Day 14

O Lord, what a glorious morning! Whether I feel on top of the world or not, I want to make the most of every minute of this new day.

Lord, I know that the greatest day of all will surely be the very last day, when this old world finally comes to an end, and you return in all your majesty and glory. And so I sometimes do genuinely pray: "Come, Lord Jesus" (Rev. 22:20). But at other times, I really hope you'll wait until I've done a few more of the things I've planned.

But, Lord, I know you've got all things in hand, so it is not for me to try to forecast when Jesus will come or to want my little plans fulfilled before he comes.

All I really want is to be close to Jesus at every stage of my life so that, whenever Jesus comes, he will welcome me as his very own friend.

Help me today to do what needs to be done. Help me do those things that will help others experience your love and care through me.

If today is to be the last day, then come, Lord Jesus. Amen.

Evening Day 14

Well, Lord, we are still here, and you have not come yet, so thanks for another day. Thanks for the time to enjoy your good creation and some more of the pleasures of life on earth.

Thank you—
- for friends who go out of their way to show kindness and love to me;
- for my family—the foundation of my life on earth;
- for my work and the sense of satisfaction it gives me each day;
- for the members of my church family, who share themselves with me and pray for me;
- for your creation with its beauty, colors, scents, and aromas, and the lovely food that I enjoy each day.

I could spend all my prayer time going on and on with that list, but I also need to spend a few moments in confessing that there are just as many of your gifts and blessings that I take for granted each day. Please forgive me for my blindness and ingratitude.

Help me go to sleep in peace, looking forward to the good day that you will give me tomorrow. In Jesus' name. Amen.

Morning   Day 15

Lord God, the darkness is over; the light of a new day has come.
  It would be wonderful if, just as easily as one can say those words, the darkness of sin and my old nature would simply vanish because the light of Jesus shines into my life. But I have come to know that growing up into Christ is not a fast process, and so I ask for the patience to take one step at a time. As I face one more day along life's way, I ask you to be with me through all the ups and downs I may face this day.

Help me—
  to keep you in mind and to draw on the joy and strength of your presence;
  to get on top of my sinful weaknesses;
  to let my new nature find expression in love for you and Christlike service to others;
  to show love to my own family, especially when things don't always go my way;
  to think more of the needs of others than my own.

So, Lord, be with me all through today, for Jesus' sake. Amen.

Evening Day 15

Lord, what a day it has been!

On days when the sun is shining, when birds are singing, and when the flowers are blooming, it's easy to be joyful and to appreciate what a wonderful world you have given us.

But then there are other days when I find it hard to think of things to be joyful about—when nothing seems to have gone right at work, or arguments have polluted the air, or special plans have fallen flat. Such days are really hard to take.

The trouble is, I usually end up taking out my frustrations and hurt feelings on those I love the most; I make life difficult for my family—and even take it out on you, Lord. Thank you for being so patient. And thank you for loving friends and family who never give up on me.

Forgive me for being so easily upset and for failing to lay my worries on you. Renew my inner peace and sense of security. I know you love me and will never let me down. That gives me hope and joy as I end this day in Jesus' saving name. Amen.

Morning   Day 16

Thanks, Lord, for the sleep and rest I enjoyed last night and for this new day that has just begun.

There are some things I have planned to do today, but I'm sure you will let some things happen that I have not planned. Help me realize that those unexpected things are also good for me, that they are a part of your loving plan to help me grow more and more like Christ in my life.

So, Lord, today I would like your help—
- to remember that I am a Christian, a precious saint in your kingdom;
- to grow in wisdom, so that I use my time well;
- to be patient when I feel that others are too demanding on me;
- to be more loving and caring when I sense that others need my help;
- to live my life so that other people will see at least a small glimpse of your light shining through me.

I ask this, Jesus, because of your saving love. Amen.

Evening　　　　　　　　　　Day 16

Thank you, Jesus, my Lord and Savior, that you have walked beside me and watched over me all day and that I am now here to talk with you again.

I confess that there were many times today—in fact, most times—when I just went on with my own plans, and I didn't give you a thought. Please forgive me for being so forgetful of your great love and care.

Forgive me all my sins at the end of this day so that I can go to sleep knowing I am at peace with God. Cover me with the robe of your righteousness, which you give me as a gift.

Without you, Jesus, I would not have real life. I realize that without you my life would be empty, just a filling up of the time with no purpose; but with you it is a real adventure, leading to new delights and discoveries in this world, until finally I can enjoy your company and share your great glory forever.

For your love's sake, hear and answer me. Amen.

Morning   Day 17

I must confess to you that there are days when I
 neglect this morning time of prayer and Bible
 reading. I know how important it is in my life
 with you that I set aside time to listen to you
 and to receive power for life and that I speak to
 you in prayer, so please help me develop a regular pattern in my routine of life.

As I go out on this new day, help me—
 to sense your presence with me during the day;
 to realize your guiding and guarding hand
  resting on me;
 to use my time carefully and constructively;
 to enjoy the gifts you give me;
 to be able to return home safely.

All this I ask for your love's sake. Amen.

Evening   Day 17

I'm here to say good night, Lord.

I'm so thankful that I belong to you; whether it is day or night, I have peace in my mind and joy in my heart.

I know it is good for me to be reminded again and again that you have made me right with God. You, Lord, have taken the guilt of all my failures on yourself; you have kept all God's laws for me and have suffered all the punishment I deserve for my sin. All through this life on earth, and then forever in the life to come, I'll never stop saying: "Thank you, Lord."

Since you've done all this for me, help me to keep the resolutions I make when I say that I want—
to do the will of God better;
to show more kindness and love to others;
to be more forgiving.
Then I'll be more like the person you want me to be.

I ask this in Jesus' name. Amen.

Morning   Day 18

A new day is here, loving God! Good morning!

As I think about the meaning of life, and try to discover where I fit in, I hear all kinds of strange comments. Some people say that we don't have to answer for what we do in life; we are to enjoy it, and it doesn't matter what we do. Others tell me it is great when you can cheat the system and get away with it. I am tempted at times to listen to such voices and to follow their advice. But I know that your Word says they are wrong. Because I am a child of God, I also agree that they are wrong.

Help me today—
> to know that I am accountable to you for what I do with the life you have given me;
> to choose the right path that I ought to follow;
> to be filled with the Holy Spirit so that I can enjoy life, doing what is good;
> to look beyond the short term so that I make the right decisions for my future.

All I want is to make sure that I continue each day with you, my Lord, until we are together always.

I pray in Jesus' name. Amen.

Evening   Day 18

Thank you, Lord, for keeping me safe all through this day. I'm sure there were many dangers from which you protected me that I wasn't even aware of. Thanks again!

As I look at my life, there are times when it seems quite clear what I should be doing, what you are calling me to do. But there are also times when I become unsettled, when I wonder whether I am taking the road that you have planned for me to take. I need and want your guidance for all my planning, dear God, but especially for those times when my choices and decisions affect the direction of the rest of my life.

Even in the small everyday events I know you are guiding me.

I want to say thank you—
> for all the friends and loved ones who bring joy to my life;
> for a healthy sense of ambition and the desire to do my work well;
> for the world of nature with all its beauty for me to enjoy.

Forgive me for the mistakes I made today, even those I'm not aware of or don't like to face truthfully. Let the blood of Jesus wash me clean, and I will go to sleep in peace. For Jesus' sake. Amen.

Morning Day 19

Some mornings the crowing of a rooster is the signal telling me that a new day has started and it's time to get up. Sometimes it is easy to get up and to be excited about the work I face and the things I've planned, but on other days I find it very hard to get out and do the things that seem very ordinary, and even rather boring.

Lord, thank you for the various signs or signals you give to help us in our lives—just as you warned Peter when he denied you three times. And just as Peter foolishly didn't listen to the warning of the first cock-crow, and he denied you, so also many times in my life I too have failed to listen and obey. I too need your second cock-crow to drive me out in shame to weep bitterly.

Alert me with a clear signal if I neglect your Word, prayer, and regular worship in God's house so that I do not fall away from you. Help me realize that it is the devil who suggests that such spiritual exercises are not necessary and that I can continue to be a Christian without them.

Keep me and all your people close to you, growing strong in the Spirit, so that we never fall away from you and lose eternal life.

I pray this in Jesus' name. Amen.

Evening Day 19

Lord, it is easy to go to bed and rest in peace when life is good, when you have a good home, love and happiness in the family, plenty of food, good clothes, and many other pleasures in life. Tonight, as I go to bed, I want to remember in my prayer those people for whom life is not very good.

Please be with those—
> who have parents who are separated;
> who are finding it hard to accept new parents;
> who have parents who are always arguing and fighting;
> who have parents who waste their money and don't have much for food;
> who don't have any friends to help them;
> who don't know Jesus and the great love of God;
> who don't realize that there is a life to come;
> who are sick—especially those having no hope of getting well again;
> who don't have even a bed to sleep in.

As I remember such people tonight, make me realize just how privileged I am—not simply because of the material blessings I enjoy, but because I am your child, redeemed by Jesus, and led by the Spirit. Let me never forget that!

I ask this all in Jesus' name. Amen.

Morning   Day 20

Lord, what a wonderful country I am living in.

I know that it's easy to find plenty of things wrong
> with our country. We growl about—
> > the government taking too much tax to provide
> > > schools, hospitals, roads, and social security;
> >
> > the prices going up all the time;
> > our wages being too small to buy all the luxuries
> > > we would like to have;
> >
> > the winter being too cold, the summer too hot.

And yet I know that there are few places in the
> world that have the living standards that we
> do. And in many countries people are losing
> their lives through terrorism, starvation, earthquakes, tornadoes, rioting, and other calamities.

Thank you, Lord, for our wonderful country. Help us
> all to appreciate your many gifts to us, so that
> we do our best to make this land a place that
> pleases both you and us.

Help all who lead our country to be wise in handling
> the affairs of our land. May they all uphold
> what is good and pleasing to you.

We ask this for Jesus' sake. Amen.

Evening   Day 20

Tonight, in my prayer I want to think about the
   needs of the people who touch my life.

Lord, you have taught me that I am meeting you as I
   meet other people. And you have said that
   when your disciples do things for other people—even the simplest things for the most
   insignificant people—we are doing them for
   you in grateful faith.

Help me, therefore, to be a "little Christ" to my
   neighbor, especially—
   to those who want to stop and talk awhile;
   to those who need a helping hand;
   to those who are worried and feel like giving in;
   to those who are in need of food and clothing;
   to those who are sick or dying;
   to those who are sad because a loved one has
      died;
   to those who don't have friends;
   to those who have no family to care for them;
   to those who don't know Jesus at all and are
      missing out on eternal life.

Now let me sleep in peace as I commend myself and
   them to your loving care, for Jesus' sake. Amen.

Morning Day 21

O God, you are our Maker and all-knowing Lord; you know us better than we know ourselves.

That worries me at times, because there are things in my life that I certainly don't want anyone else to know about. When I realize that you know all about them, I feel very guilty. How thankful and relieved I am to know that when I confess those things to you and ask for mercy, you forgive and get rid of them, just as an eraser rubs a blackboard clean. You've even said that you take them right out of your memory forever.

Loving God, assure me of that again this morning so that I am not troubled by my past mistakes and can make a new start in serving you. Send me out to this new day, certain of your love, to do my very best.

Help me—
- to find joy and satisfaction in all I do;
- to be careful with my words so that I help and do not hurt;
- to hear any call for help that you want me to hear;
- to live in such a way that I'm not a burden to others.

All this I ask for Jesus' sake. Amen.

Evening   Day 21

As your disciple, Lord, I promise to do my very
best; but when the day is ended and I look
back, I wonder how much of the day has really
been my best.

Please forgive my failures.

Where I have been—
    slack in my work,
    disrespectful to people placed over me,
    proud of myself and scornful of others,
    slow to give help to those who needed it,
    impatient with other people,
    unthankful, selfish, or just a nuisance to others,

I am truly sorry and ask for your pardon and renewing power. Wash away all my sins, and make me clean and acceptable to you.

Watch over me and all my family and friends this night. Bless us all with the calmness and peace that comes from living in your saving love. Amen.

Morning　　　　　　　　　　Day 22

Heavenly Lord, there are times when I feel very
strong, full of trust and confidence in you. At
those times I feel that I could do great things—
even move mountains, as Jesus said. Thank you
for faith, your precious gift to me.

But sometimes my faith seems to flicker, and I
become troubled. I even wonder whether I'll be
able to keep with you right to the end. If I rely
on myself, I know I'll fall away from you; but
deep down I know you want to keep me in the
faith by your Spirit and that he can win out
over my weakness.

Help me this day—
  to remain strong in faith;
  to believe that you can do all things for me;
  to be sure that I am still your child, as I've been
    since my baptism;
  to face the challenges of life, confident that you
    are there to help me win the victory when
    I'm tempted to go wrong.

Keep my heart joyful throughout the day as I count
all the blessings you give me, and give you
praise and thanks for all of them.

All these things I ask for Jesus' sake. Amen.

Evening Day 22

At the close of this day, dear Lord, let my mind and spirit rest in you. Let me put off all my cares and worries and lay them on you, because you have said that you care for me.

When Jesus says that there is no need for me to get upset or worried, because you take care of everything—the flowers, the birds, and even the hairs on my head—it sounds so easy. I know that worry spoils my life, and I know how my worry upsets those people who love me. And yet I still let things worry me.

Lord, I'm not asking for a special supply of the self-confidence or self-assurance that we hear so much about in today's world, but rather for the ability to put all my cares in your hands and to grow in the confidence that you are in control of both this world and my life and that there is nothing for me to be scared of. You have promised that the Holy Spirit will keep me trusting in you and give me a stronger faith.

Let me have this gift as I go to sleep in your name. Amen.

Morning   Day 23

Each new day comes, Lord, and soon it is gone. Some days are rather full of interesting and exciting things; others are very ordinary, and some even boring. Since life is a mixture of all kinds of days and events, keep me remembering that you are guiding all things for my good.

As I go out to face this day, keep me aware of how easy it is to get caught up in this world's mad rush to get rich in money and material things. You have said: "Will a person gain anything if he wins the whole world but is himself lost or defeated? Of course not!" I don't ever want to be lost or defeated. So lead me more and more to understand what it means to forget self, to take up my cross, and to follow you.

By your Spirit, enable me to grow in being the kind of person you want me to be so that my life is a good witness to your saving love, and gives glory to God.

Hear my prayer, Lord Jesus! Amen.

Evening   Day 23

Tonight, dear Lord, as the day ends, I want to say a big thank you for all I enjoyed today and for all my life up to this moment.

As I go to sleep, I want to think about the many people who work to provide my needs and enrich my life.

Thank you—
>   for my loving family, who help supply my needs and who love me even when I'm rather difficult to live with;
>   for the people who work with me;
>   for the doctors and nurses who care for us when we are sick;
>   for the musicians who bring us the pleasures of music;
>   for the announcers, actors, and artists who inform or entertain us;
>   for the police, firefighters, and ambulance workers, who are always on the alert to come to our aid.

As I call to mind those who have an influence on my life, I realize how much I depend on other people, and how much you have provided for me. Help me show my thankfulness to all who help me. And help us all live in your love, for Jesus' sake. Amen.

Morning   Day 24

Lord in this morning hour, I want to focus my
    thoughts on my church, into which you have
    placed me ever since my baptism.

First of all, I want to say a thank you—
    for my caring pastor (even if the sermons some-
        times go on a bit long) who wants to help me
        stay close to Jesus and remain in God's
        kingdom forever;
    for the faithful members who are "there every
        Sunday," and who are trying to make sure that
        our church remains alive and active;
    for the people, young and old, who are busy
        encouraging others in faith and helping them
        enjoy fun and fellowship in the family of God,
    for the building we call the house of God, where
        we can go on Sunday, feel the presence of God,
        and sing his praises with others;
    for the Word of God, which leads me on the
        right path through this life to the next.

I also want to say "I'm sorry" for times when I forget—
    to go to church,
    to pray for others in my church family,
    and to care for those who have needed my help.

Please accept this my prayer for Jesus' sake. Amen.

Evening Day 24

There are times, dear Lord, when I wonder whether my Christian life is just a matter of a lot of words, nothing more than empty promises and good resolutions. I'm sure that if getting to heaven depended on good intentions, I would pass with flying colors.

But I want to get beyond words and promises, down to deeds and actions. And I don't want to hate myself for my past neglect in good deeds, for you have told me that is wrong; I claim the forgiveness you freely offer me through Jesus.

Now that I am clean, I want to start again with the help of your Spirit. Help me to drown my old sinful nature and to put on the new creation, like Jesus himself, so that I keep those good resolutions I make rather often.

When the Holy Spirit fills me with his power, I know great things will begin to happen. Other people will also be surprised at what God is doing with this very ordinary me. Then we will all give thanks and praise to God.

Let this happen in my life, for Jesus' sake. Amen.

Morning　　　　　　　　　　Day 25

Lord, each day fills me with expectations. Let such expectations be realistic as I go out to this new day.

Help me—
- to realize that you do not expect the impossible of me;
- to accept that I am an ordinary human being with weaknesses that need forgiveness from you and others;
- to remember that others are also imperfect human beings with weaknesses that need my forgiveness;
- to recognize that others are more likely to be honest with me when I open myself to them;
- to divide up my time wisely for working, resting, playing, loving, and serving.

Thank you, Lord, for this new day. Help me now to use its hours wisely so that at its end I may have become a little more like the person you want me to be.

For Jesus' sake. Amen.

Evening   Day 25

As this day ends, I recall the thought of the evening hymn that says, as Christians, we should dread the grave as little as our bed.

Dear God, if Jesus had not rescued us from our sin and its punishment, we would be terribly afraid of dying. But on Easter Jesus destroyed the curse of death, and so we are no longer afraid. He tells us that our names are written in the book of life, so our spirits are lifted up in the certainty of being forever with the Lord.

Tonight I commend to you—
> those who are afraid of death;
> those who don't know Jesus or what real life with God means;
> those who are suffering great pain;
> those who are terminally ill, especially those who are suffering alone and without any peace with God;
> those who don't want to open their lives to God;
> those who are living in great fear.

Lord, help these people come to you. Give us all your peace, the peace that passes all understanding because Jesus has made peace for us with God.

In his name I offer my prayer at day's end. Amen.

Morning   Day 26

I thank you, Lord, for another day, for life, health, and strength. I thank you also for my new life in Christ. Help me use all those gifts to your glory.

As I go out to my daily work, I want to do what you want me to do, because your will is always good. I can never offer you perfect obedience—as Jesus did when he was on this earth—but I do want to know you more clearly, love you more dearly, and follow you more nearly day by day.

So, help me each day—
> to hear your Word and think deeply upon it to discover your will for me;
> to be willing to listen to other people of God who can help me learn your will;
> to be understanding toward those who need to correct me in my work or behavior;
> to be endlessly patient with those who irritate me.

Above all, renew my faith and my love for you, so that I keep on wanting to obey you and do your will here on earth as it is done in heaven.

Help us all do this for Jesus' sake. Amen.

Evening   Day 26

As I look back over the day, there are some things that please me greatly, and other things that make me unhappy and ashamed.

Forgive me where I went wrong—
> when I was critical of others, forgetting your warning that you will judge people the same way they judge others;
> when I was more concerned about my own comforts and needs than those of others;
> when I worried about things, instead of coming to you in prayer;
> when I forgot to share your love in the opportunities given to me;
> when I lost my temper and said words that were not very nice;
> when I forgot to give my help to someone who was hurting.

Without you, Jesus, I would be lost; but through you my sin is covered, and all is well. Thank you, dear Savior, for your love to me.

Watch over us all tonight as we go to rest. Let your peace descend upon us, especially upon those who are distressed in body, mind, or spirit.

I ask this for your love's sake. Amen.

Morning   Day 27

Dear God, when you made us and put us in this world, it was your will and plan that people live in harmony with one another. But when I read the paper and watch television, I often wonder whether people are any different from the wild animals who snarl and growl at each other and even eat one another. It seems that our world of people is always in danger of starting a new war—one which probably will destroy us all in the process.

This morning, I want to pray for our world—
>   that its leaders rule with good common sense and justice;
>   that those in authority not abuse their power;
>   that the prosperous nations act to feed the hungry and to help poor nations improve their food production;
>   that countries continue to give people the freedom to worship God;
>   that all nations allow missionaries to bring the good news of salvation in Jesus to all their people.

There are many other needs, but these are the important ones.

Bless us all as individuals and as nations, for you are our good and gracious Lord. Amen.

Evening   Day 27

Living with other people is not always easy, Lord. We have differences of opinion, and sometimes that leads to arguments. It's hard for me to stay calm and not lose my temper with some people. Forgive me for my lack of self-control.

Jesus, you have reminded us that, if we are bringing our gift to you and remember that we have not made peace with someone, we are to leave our gift there and first make peace. Wherever there is any need for me to make that peace with anyone, give me the desire and the courage to go, and the wisdom to use the right words.

Thank you also for that deep peace you have given me because you have done everything to make me right with God.

As I go to sleep, help me relax in body and mind, and hand all my worries over to you. I am ready to give all my fears and troubles to you, for I am sure that you are in full control and make all things good for those who love you. I pray in Jesus' name. Amen.

Morning   Day 28

In this morning hour, Lord, as I begin a new day, I
  want to remember how great you are and what
  marvelous things you have already done for me
  in my life.

So, Lord, this morning I ask—
  for a good sense of balance,
    so that I can distinguish between what is
      important and what is not important, and so
      that I don't get too upset about things that
      don't matter;
  for a good sense of humor,
    so that I can learn to laugh easily and be able
      especially to laugh at myself and not get
      angry when others laugh at me;
  for a good sense of other people's feelings,
    so that I am aware when others are silently
      crying and pine for my comfort, or when I
      am the thoughtless cause of their pain, and
      must seek their forgiveness;
  for a good sense of responsibility,
    so that I do my work, not just to please the
      boss, or to get money, but to please God;
  for a good sense of the presence of Jesus,
    so that I might go through this day in the
      company of my best friend and Lord, Jesus.

In his name I pray. Amen.

Evening   Day 28

Hello, Lord! Today is now over, and I come to you
to thank you for looking after me throughout
this day. Though you already know my
thoughts, I don't want to use that as an excuse
for not talking to you.

During today there were many fatal accidents—
on the roads, in the water, and even in the air. I
get really sad that so many lives are wasted.
Comfort all those who have lost loved ones.

You obviously must have a purpose in letting such
things happen, but that reason is often not
clear to us. Remind me to trust you and not to
worry about the reason.

Lord, when people die so suddenly, it only helps
remind me that my time on this earth is very
limited and that I should be prepared at all
times to leave this life.

Always help me to spend my time usefully, knowing
that you have a special purpose for me while I
am here on earth.

I pray this in your name, dear Savior, for by your
cross you have given me real purpose in life
now and the assurance of life forever. Amen.

Morning　　　　　　　　　　　Day 29

Before I get too busy with work today, I want to spend this time talking to you, my Lord, about friends.

How terrible life must be for those people who have no friends. I thank you, Lord, that I am able to enjoy life with many friends, in our family, at my work, in our community, and at my church. I especially appreciate the friendship with Christians in our church family, where we listen to your Word together, pray together, work together, and enjoy fun together.

If there are any people who need a friend, show me how I can be that friend, and help me to be the friend you want me to be.

Forgive me if I have failed to be a good friend to those who depend on me.

Most of all I want to thank you, Jesus, for being my best friend. Without you, I would not have any real peace or happiness with God. Give me your kind of love to share with all my other friends. For your love's sake. Amen.

Evening   Day 29

Dear Lord, it is really wonderful to live in the assurance that for me all is right with you because I have met Jesus Christ, your Son, and have put my trust in him.

Thank you—
- for anything that happened today that helped me grow a little wiser;
- for the usual people at home and at work who helped this day run smoothly;
- for the new people I met who helped make today a little different;
- for the opportunities you gave me to see and do the good things you have planned for me to do;
- for all the pleasures of life that I often take for granted.

You have promised that, while I sleep, your holy angels watch over me to keep away all evil from me. Watch over me now and give me your peace and forgiveness. For Jesus' sake. Amen.

Morning   Day 30

Hello, Lord! I love the chance for this little talk with you, and I want to thank you for being able to speak with you and for knowing that you are listening. You have told us that, even when we don't know what to say or say our prayers in an imperfect way, your Spirit pleads for us and even corrects our prayers.

Thank you also for the way you guide me through the voice of my conscience. Please sharpen my conscience by the power of your Spirit, as I read and study your Word, so that I can see more clearly what is right and what is wrong. Most of all, when my conscience is troubled by the evil I've done, give me real peace of mind as I bring my sins to Jesus, confess them, and ask his forgiveness. Send me on my way absolutely sure that he has taken my sin and washed me clean through his blood shed on the cross.

I have never deserved such great love, but it is mine forever.

Lord, let your great love grow in me so I can share it will all those people with whom I live and work.

All this I ask for your love's sake. Amen.

Evening   Day 30

Isn't it wonderful to be free? Lord, I praise you for
   giving us real freedom in our country: freedom
   to carry out our own plans, to have personal
   possessions and property, to enjoy recreation,
   to elect our leaders and to be able to criticize
   them, to worship God in church as our
   conscience directs.

I praise you most of all that I can stand free in front
   of you, my God. I've been set free from
   measuring up to your perfect standards because
   Jesus did that perfectly in my place.

I'm free now to discover the best kind of life that
   you want for me. Led by your Spirit, I am free
   to enjoy all your good gifts and to serve you
   and my neighbor with all that I am and have.

Lord, don't let me ever lose that great freedom, for
   you won it for us by Jesus' cross, death, and
   resurrection. Amen.

Morning　　　　　　　　　　Day 31

Lord, you've called me to be your disciple. There are many days when I feel that you didn't make a very good choice:
 I forget to do your will;
 I don't remember to tell others of your gift of salvation;
 I feel too scared to let others know I'm a Christian;
 I get angry too quickly;
 I lose my patience;
 I say some rather nasty things.

Perhaps I'll never be a good disciple; maybe I ought to give up.

Whenever I feel so useless, set me straight again with words I like to hear, such as:
 "God has chosen you, not to demand a great performance of you, but out of love for you;
 "God understands your feelings of failure and forgives you. God will help you do things better in the future;
 "Don't ever give up. God never gives up on you."

Thanks for those words of comfort and encouragement. I love you, Jesus. Amen.

Evening Day 31

My Lord, as I come into your presence this evening to speak with you, I realize that time is always moving on. The days go by, and soon a month and then a year has gone. Help me to keep aware of time, so that I learn to use it wisely, and never waste it on useless things.

As I take off my clothes to go to sleep, help me to put off the old human nature and all my sins of the day gone by.

Savior Jesus, you died to take away that great burden, you made me clean with your precious blood, and you can cover me all over with your perfect holiness. Bless me again with your saving gifts so that my loving God will say: "You, my child, are a saint, fit for the kingdom of heaven."

That's really all I want tonight. Then I have that wonderful peace of yours, which passes all our human understanding. Give that peace to all your people as we go to sleep this night.

Lord Jesus, I pray this in your precious saving name. Amen.

PERSONAL PRAYERS FOR GROWING CHRISTIANS

Copyright © 1986 by Openbook Publishers

Dimensions for Living edition published 2002

All rights reserved.
No part of this work may be reproduced or transmitted in any form or by any means, electronic or mechanical, including photocopying and recording, or by any information storage or retrieval system, except as may be expressly permitted by the 1976 Copyright Act or in writing from the publisher. Requests for permission should be addressed to Dimensions for Living, P.O. Box 801, 201 Eighth Avenue South, Nashville, TN 37202-0801.

This book is printed on acid-free paper.

ISBN 0-687-06317-5

All Scripture quotations are taken from the *Holy Bible: New International Version®*. Copyright © 1973, 1978, 1984 by the International Bible Society. Used by permission of Zondervan Publishing House. All rights reserved.

Some of these prayers originally appeared in a slightly longer form in the Openbook Publishers edition.

02 03 04 05 06 07 08 09 10 11—10 9 8 7 6 5 4 3 2 1

MANUFACTURED IN THE UNITED STATES OF AMERICA